Dark Experiments on Humans

25 real cases in history

Phillips Tahuer

Ediciones Afrodita

Contents:

Introduction

*"Science never solves a problem without
creating 10 more."*
George Bernard Shaw

The history of human experimentation between the 19th and 21st centuries is a complex and often disturbing narrative marked by major scientific advances, profound ethical violations, and subsequent reforms. This period witnessed a wide range of experiments performed on human subjects, many of which were carried out without informed consent and under exploitative conditions. These experiments, while contributing to medical and scientific knowledge, also highlight the dark side of research practices and the persistent challenge of ensuring ethical standards in human studies.

From the first vaccination trials conducted by Edward Jenner in the late 18th century, which lacked informed consent, to the horrific experiments conducted by Nazi doctors during World War II, the 19th and early 20th centuries are replete with examples of human suffering under the guise of scientific research.

The unethical exploitation of vulnerable populations during this era underscored the need for strict ethical guidelines, ultimately leading to the establishment of the Nuremberg Code in 1947, which emphasized voluntary consent as a fundamental principle.

Despite these legislative advances, ethical violations continued, particularly in the United States, where experiments often targeted marginalized groups, including racial minorities and prisoners, as seen in the infamous Tuskegee syphilis study.

The mid-20th century was characterized by a series of controversial military and government experiments, including chemical and radioactive exposure tests, often conducted without proper consent and with significant harm to participants.

Revulsion at these abuses prompted other regulatory frameworks such as the Declaration of Helsinki (1964), although its implementation remained inconsistent and many subjects were not informed or compensated for their participation in various scientific experiments.

Notably, the 1971 Stanford Prison Experiment and the CIA's Project QKHILLTOP exemplified current ethical dilemmas in psychological and pharmacological research, raising critical questions about the balance between scientific discovery and human rights.

Even in the 21st century, the legacy of unethical human experimentation continues to cast a large shadow. Modern examples of medical misconduct, often reflecting institutional and racial bias, reveal that issues of consent and exploitation are far from resolved.

While historical abuses have led to important ethical reforms, the ongoing debate over the use of data obtained from unethical experiments illustrates the persistent struggle to reconcile scientific progress with moral responsibility.

Thus, the history of human experimentation serves as a stark reminder of the critical importance of ethical oversight in safeguarding the well-being and rights of research participants.

19th Century Human Experiments

The 19th century was a period of significant advances in medical and scientific knowledge. However, this era also saw numerous controversial and often unethical experiments conducted on human subjects.

• Early Vaccination Trials

One of the most notable examples of 19th-century human experimentation is the work of English surgeon Edward Jenner. In 1796, Jenner conducted the world's first vaccination trial by exposing his gardener's 8-year-old son to cowpox and subsequently smallpox. This human challenge trial laid the groundwork for modern immunology, but it was conducted without what would today be considered proper informed consent.

• Exploitation of vulnerable populations

Throughout the 19th century, many medical professionals saw "opportunities" to perform experiments on gullible, vulnerable, or desperate individuals. These experiments often lacked real scientific value and were motivated more by professional curiosity than a desire to advance medical knowledge.

The history of medicine during this period is marked by numerous instances in which physicians exploited their patients, resulting in significant human suffering.

Impact on medical ethics

The unethical practices of the 19th century have had a lasting impact on the field of medical ethics. These early experiments highlighted the need for stricter ethical guidelines to protect human subjects in medical research. While the concept of informed consent and ethical review committees had not yet been established, the controversial nature of these experiments laid the groundwork for future reforms in medical research ethics.

Early 20th Century Human Experiments

The early 20th century saw a number of controversial and often unethical human experiments, despite the creation of ethical guidelines such as the Nuremberg Code in 1947. The Nuremberg trials of 1945–46, which prosecuted Nazi doctors for unethical human experiments during World War II, initiated public debate over the ethics of human subjects research. The Nuremberg Code, established in 1947, differentiated between therapeutic and nontherapeutic experimentation, and in its first provision stated that "the voluntary consent of the human subject is absolutely essential."

However, this code had little impact in the United States, where doctors saw it as irrelevant to their research because of the promise of antibiotics and increasing federal funding.

Despite these ethical guidelines, numerous human experiments were conducted unethically from the 1940s through the 1970s. These included experiments with radiation, toxic exposures to Agent Orange during the Vietnam War, and other lesser-known studies of chemical warfare preparedness.

Human experimentation during this period often involved men, women, and children, including infants, the elderly, and pregnant women, both within the facilities and among the surrounding populations. Subjects included common criminals, captured bandits, political prisoners, the homeless, and the mentally handicapped.

Victims were not limited to any specific group but included a variety of ethnicities and nationalities, such as Chinese, Russians, Mongolians, Koreans, and occasionally Europeans and Americans.

One of the most notorious units involved in these experiments was Unit 731, which conducted tests with numerous biological agents, including anthrax, typhoid, and plague. The unit's activities were part of Japan's biological warfare efforts during World War II, which affected both military personnel and civilians.

In the postwar period, the United States conducted its investigation into these crimes and produced several reports detailing the extent of human experiments conducted by Unit 731.

The outcry over these abuses led to the development of the Nuremberg Code of Medical Ethics. However, the code was not cited in the verdicts against the defendants in the doctors' trial and was not incorporated into German or American medical law.

Despite the establishment of these ethical guidelines, the history of medical experimentation in the early 20th century is marked by numerous violations, raising questions about the application and effectiveness of ethical standards in protecting human subjects.

Mid-20th Century Human Experiments

The mid-20th century in the United States was marked by significant scientific advances and medical discoveries. This era witnessed the rapid expansion of medical knowledge and techniques, which encouraged medical professionals to conduct numerous experiments on human subjects to better understand the human body or test the efficacy of treatments. These human experiments, largely directed and funded by the United States government, were often conducted in unethical or illegal ways. Although the Nuremberg Code and the Declaration of Helsinki were introduced to protect the rights and welfare of human subjects in medical research, unethical experimentation continued over the next few decades in the United States.

Unethical Experiments in the United States

One of the most notorious examples of unethical human experimentation was the Tuskegee Syphilis Study, which in 1972 raised alarm bells about the misuse of human subjects. This study contributed to the enactment of the National Research Act, which was intended to protect human subjects in medical research. During World War II, the United States government conducted mustard gas experiments on American soldiers to test the effectiveness of protective clothing and equipment in the event of mustard gas attacks. Soldiers were placed in gas chambers or directly exposed to mustard gas for hours without their informed or voluntary consent, resulting in severe respiratory problems, skin burns, and subsequent cancers.

Race-Based Experiments and Other Unethical Practices

From the 1940s to the 1970s, numerous scientific experiments were conducted on human subjects, despite the Nuremberg Code. These included experiments with radiation and toxic exposures, such as Agent Orange during the Vietnam War. The experiments on human subjects involved men, women, and children, including infants, the elderly, and pregnant women. Subjects included common criminals, political prisoners, homeless people, and the mentally handicapped. Ordinary citizens were also victims of these experiments, conducted both within the facilities and among the surrounding populations.

Nazi Human Experimentation

Nazi human experimentation, a series of medical experiments conducted on prisoners by Nazi Germany, was primarily carried out between 1942 and 1945 in concentration camps. These experiments, led by figures such as Sigmund Rascher and Eduard Wirths, were intended to aid German military personnel, develop new weapons, and promote Nazi racial ideology and eugenics. The experiments included freezing and hypothermia tests to simulate conditions on the Eastern Front and high-altitude experiments to aid German pilots. These experiments resulted in numerous deaths and serious permanent injuries among the subjects.

Post-World War II Period and the Cold War

After World War II, the Cold War led to more unethical experiments. For example, Fort Detrick in Maryland became the headquarters for U.S. biological warfare experiments. Operation Whitecoat involved the injection of infectious agents into military forces to observe their effects. Public outrage over these government experiments led to several congressional investigations and hearings, although no prosecutions resulted. Many of the subjects who participated in these trials were not compensated or informed that they had participated in such experiments.

These human experiments from the mid-20th century highlight the ethical challenges and human rights violations inherent in scientific research during that period. The resulting ethical standards and guidelines aimed to prevent such abuses in future medical research.

Human Experiments of the Late 20th Century

The late 20th century saw a number of controversial and ethically dubious human experiments, despite international regulations intended to protect human subjects in research.

One of the most notorious cases was the Tuskegee Syphilis Study, which was made public in 1972. This study, conducted by the United States Public Health Service, followed African-American men infected with syphilis without providing them with adequate treatment, even after penicillin became available.

In this same vein, various unethical experiments were conducted on military personnel without their consent. For example, soldiers were often subjected to tests involving toxic exposures, such as Agent Orange during the Vietnam War, and to radiation experiments.

In the field of psychology, the Stanford Prison Experiment, conducted in 1971 at Stanford University, investigated the psychological effects of perceived power by assigning volunteers the roles of prisoners and guards in a simulated prison environment.

In 1954, the CIA initiated Project QKHILLTOP to study Chinese brainwashing techniques and develop new interrogation methods. Dr. Harold Wolff of Cornell University led this research, which included experiments with drugs and brain-damaging procedures on human subjects, often without their consent.

Ethical Lessons

The ethical violations committed in these late 20th-century experiments highlight the critical importance of ethical oversight in research involving human subjects. The researchers stress that while these studies offer valuable lessons, they must be conducted with rigorous ethical standards to protect the rights and well-being of participants.

Human Experiments in the 21st Century

In the 21st century, despite numerous ethical guidelines and regulatory frameworks, controversial experiments on human subjects have continued to be conducted. These experiments often expose the persistent problems surrounding consent, exploitation, and harm in scientific research.

The legacy of medical malpractice has persisted into the 21st century, often reflecting deep-rooted institutional and racial biases. For example, the removal of an offensive statue in New York City in 2018 symbolized an attempt to redress historical abuses. The statue depicted a 19th-century gynecologist who had notoriously experimented on enslaved women under the false premise that black people did not feel pain.

This historical context highlights the continuing impact of unethical practices of the past on modern society.

Human experimentation has also been affected by racially discriminatory practices. This led to the passage of the National Research Act in 1974.

This act was a response to the broader recognition of unethical practices targeting marginalized groups, revealing the extent to which scientific research had historically exploited vulnerable populations.

Ethical Deliberations

The ethical debate surrounding the use of data obtained from unethical experiments remains a contentious issue. Some scholars argue that the use of unethically obtained information perpetuates the wrongs inflicted on victims, while others believe that such data can still have scientific value if managed responsibly.

This debate highlights the ongoing struggle to balance scientific progress with ethical responsibility.

To conclude this introduction to the topic, it is worth highlighting, so as never to forget, who is considered the most feared and dark figure in modern science; we refer to Josef Mengele:

The Life of Josef Mengele and His War Crimes

Josef Mengele, known as the "Angel of Death", was a Nazi doctor who carried out atrocious medical experiments on prisoners at the Auschwitz concentration camp during World War II.

Josef Mengele is synonymous with cruelty and barbarity in the history of the Holocaust. His inhuman experiments and disregard for human life represent the worst of Nazi ideology.

Josef Mengele was born on March 16, 1911, in Günzburg, Germany, to a well-to-do family. He studied medicine and anthropology at the universities of Munich, Bonn, and Frankfurt, earning his doctorate in 1938. His early academic work focused on genetics and racial anthropology, interests that would later translate into his horrific experiments at Auschwitz.

Mengele joined the SA (Sturmabteilung) in 1933 and the NSDAP (Nazi Party) in 1937. In 1938, he joined the SS (Schutzstaffel), where he quickly rose through the ranks. His military career and fervent belief in Nazi ideology led him to Auschwitz, where he found the stage for his monstrous activities.

In May 1943, Mengele was assigned to Auschwitz, where he soon became known for his role in the "selections" at the train ramp, deciding who would be sent to forced labor and who to the gas chambers.

Mengele performed a number of heinous medical experiments, particularly targeting twins, people with deformities, and other prisoners. These experiments included:

<u>Twin Experiments</u>: Mengele was obsessed with twins, whom he subjected to cruel procedures, such as injections of chemicals, amputations, and blood transfusions between twins.

<u>Genetic Abnormality Experiments</u>: He performed brutal studies on prisoners with dwarfism and other deformities, attempting to understand and manipulate genetic characteristics.

<u>Lethal Injections and Surgeries</u>: Mengele injected toxic substances into prisoners' eyes to change their color and performed surgeries without anesthesia to study the human body.

Mengele's experiments were not only devoid of scientific value but also resulted in the death and mutilation of thousands of prisoners. His cruelty and the arbitrary nature of his experiments made him a feared and hated figure in Auschwitz.

At the end of World War II, Mengele fled Auschwitz and spent time in various prisoner-of-war camps without being identified. In 1949, with the help of a network of Nazi sympathizers, he escaped to South America, first to Argentina and then to Paraguay and Brazil.

In South America, Mengele lived under various aliases and managed to evade capture for decades. He continued to work in various occupations, from farmer to merchant, and maintained contact with other escaped Nazis.

Josef Mengele died on February 7, 1979, in Brazil, apparently drowned while swimming. His identity was confirmed in 1985 through forensic testing, closing a chapter of decades of searching and speculation.

Mengele was charged with war crimes, crimes against humanity, and genocide for his activities at Auschwitz. However, he was never brought to justice due to his ability to evade capture.

Mengele has become a symbol of the cruelty of the Holocaust. His name and actions are remembered in museums, memorials, and survivor testimonies, ensuring that the atrocities he committed are never forgotten.

Controversial Experiments

Experiments on humans have been essential to the progress of medicine and science. However, a lack of regulations and ethical oversight in the past led to abuses and atrocities in the name of knowledge. Below is a selection of the most infamous and dark experiments on the human body and mind, highlighting the lack of regulations under which they were carried out.

1. The Kellogg Experiment

Carried out in the 1930s by psychologist Winthrop Niles Kellogg and his wife Luella Kellogg, it is a fascinating and controversial study in the history of psychology and comparative ethology. This experiment aimed to explore the learning and developmental capabilities of a chimpanzee compared to a human child, providing valuable (though sometimes disputed) insights into the nature of intelligence and behavior.

During the first decades of the 20th century, psychologists and biologists were deeply interested in understanding the nature of human and animal intelligence. Behaviorist theories, which dominated psychology at the time, focused on studying observable behavior and its relationship to the environment. In this context, Winthrop Niles Kellogg, a professor of psychology at Indiana University, decided to conduct an innovative experiment to investigate the similarities and differences between humans and apes.

The experiment began in 1931 when the Kelloggs decided to raise a chimpanzee, named Gua, with their son Donald, who was about the same age as the chimpanzee. Gua was adopted by the Kelloggs when she was seven months old, and Donald was ten months old at the time. Over a period of nine months, both were treated almost identically in a controlled environment.

The main objective was to observe how the human environment affected the cognitive and behavioral development of the chimpanzee compared to the human child. Both subjects of the study were exposed to the same stimuli, including games, social interactions, and learning tasks. They were dressed the same, given the same amount of affection, and instructed in the same way. The Kelloggs meticulously recorded Gua and Donald's responses to various stimuli, including their problem-solving abilities, language development, and social behaviors.

Throughout the experiment, the Kelloggs observed several similarities and differences between Gua and Donald:

<u>Motor and Cognitive Development</u>: Initially, Gua outperformed Donald on several motor and cognitive tasks. For example, Gua was faster at learning to use utensils and solve simple mechanical problems. However, this advantage began to diminish over time as Donald developed his skills.

<u>Linguistic Development:</u> One of the most significant differences observed was in language development. Despite being exposed to a human environment, Gua failed to develop language skills comparable to Donald's. Donald began to speak, while Gua could only imitate sounds without understanding their meaning.

<u>Social Behavior:</u> Both showed similar social behaviors in some aspects, such as play and interaction with adults. However, differences in their biological nature eventually became apparent, especially in the way they interacted with the environment and humans.

Overall, Gua's development was remarkable. She paid attention to commands and obeyed them better than her "human brother," went to the bathroom alone, and acquired the ability to eat with cutlery more quickly.

It was remarkable how the chimpanzee developed human skills, such as giving kisses and apologizing. Without realizing it, Gua had become the leader, who began teaching Donald typical ape skills. This alarmed the Kelloggs, who decided to end the experiment three months before the one-year deadline.

The Kellogg experiment provided valuable information about comparative cognitive and behavioral development between humans and apes. However, it also raised ethical and scientific controversies. The nature of the experiment raised questions about the subjects' well-being, especially with regard to Gua. Raising a chimpanzee in a human environment can cause identity and adjustment problems for both the animal and the humans involved.

In addition, the results of the experiment were interpreted in various ways. Some scientists argued that the observed differences supported the idea that human intelligence is unique and cannot be replicated in other species. Others suggested that the environment plays a crucial role in the development of cognitive abilities, and that, given enough time and effort, an ape could develop more advanced skills.

Despite the controversies, the Kellogg experiment remains a seminal study in the history of psychology and ethology. It highlighted the importance of the environment in cognitive development and provided a foundation for future research into animal and human intelligence. It also underscored the need to carefully consider the ethical implications of comparative studies between humans and animals.

The legacy of the Kellogg experiment lies in its contribution to our understanding of the mind and behavior, as well as its role in the evolution of ethical norms in scientific research. Through this study, scientists have learned to approach complex questions about the nature of intelligence and development with greater sensitivity and rigor.

2. The Experiments of Unit 731

Unit 731, a division of the Imperial Japanese Army during World War II, is known for the heinous human experiments it performed on prisoners. These experiments included vivisections, biological weapons testing, and exposure to lethal diseases.

During World War II, while the world was in a state of extreme conflict, some of the most inhumane and cruel research in human history was carried out by Unit 731 of the Imperial Japanese Army. Founded for the purpose of developing biological weapons, Unit 731 operated in almost total secrecy, performing brutal experiments on thousands of prisoners, primarily Chinese, but also Russians, Koreans, and Mongolians.

Unit 731 was established in 1936 in the occupied region of Manchuria, under the direction of General Shiro Ishii, a military doctor with an obsessive interest in bacteriological research. The primary goals of Unit 731 were to develop biological weapons and study their effects on the human body, in order to use them in warfare.

Experiment Methodology:

Vivisections and Surgical Experimentation
One of the most horrendous aspects of Unit 731 was the practice of vivisections on living prisoners. These procedures were performed without anesthesia to study the effects of various diseases and injuries on the human body. Prisoners were deliberately infected with pathogens such as anthrax, plague, and cholera, and

then dissected alive to observe the progression of these diseases internally.

Biological Weapons Testing

Unit 731 conducted extensive biological weapons testing. They released fleas infected with bubonic plague over Chinese cities, causing devastating epidemics. They also contaminated water wells and food with pathogenic bacteria to study the spread and effects of these diseases on the population.

Freezing Experiments

Prisoners were subjected to freezing experiments to understand how the human body responds to hypothermia. Subjects were forced to remain in extremely cold temperatures, and their extremities were immersed in ice-cold water until they froze. Researchers then studied the effects of the thawing process, often causing unimaginable pain and death.

Chemical Weapons Testing

In addition to biological weapons, Unit 731 also experimented with chemical weapons. Prisoners were exposed to mustard gas and other toxic chemicals to study their effects. These experiments resulted in severe burns, internal injuries, and death.

Venereal Disease Studies

Prisoners, including women, were deliberately infected with venereal diseases such as syphilis and gonorrhea to study the progression and effects of these infections. These studies included forced sexual experiments between infected and uninfected prisoners.

The horrors of Unit 731 came to light after the war, but many of those responsible never faced justice. At the end of the war, US authorities offered immunity in exchange for the research data collected by Unit 731, allowing many of the scientists and doctors involved to evade punishment.

The legacy of Unit 731 is a grim reminder of the atrocities that can occur when science and medicine stray from ethics and humanity. These events underlined the need for strict ethical regulations in weapons research and development, as well as the importance of remembering and learning from history to avoid repeating the mistakes of the past.

3. The Tuskegee Syphilis Study

The Tuskegee Syphilis Study conducted between 1932 and 1972, is one of the most notorious examples of ethical violations in medical research in the United States.

This research program, conducted by the United States Public Health Service (PHS), is remembered as one of the greatest ethical lapses in the history of medicine. Over the course of 40 years, the study observed the progression of syphilis in African-American men without providing treatment, even after penicillin became the standard cure for the disease.

In the 1930s, syphilis was a common and devastating disease. The medical community was interested in understanding its natural progression. In this context, PHS, together with the Tuskegee Institute and Dr. Taliaferro Clark, launched the Tuskegee Syphilis Study in Macon County, Alabama, a region with a high prevalence of syphilis among the African-American population.

The stated goal of the study was to observe the natural history of untreated syphilis in African-American men. The researchers wanted to better understand the different stages of the disease and its long-term effects on the human body.

The study recruited 600 African-American men, 399 with syphilis and 201 without the disease, as a control group. The participants were mostly poor, illiterate farmers. The men were promised free medical treatment, transportation to the clinic, daily meals, and burial insurance.

Initially, the treatment available in the 1930s for syphilis was toxic and of limited effectiveness. However, after penicillin was established as the effective cure in the 1940s, the study's researchers deliberately withheld treatment for the participants. The men were denied information about their diagnosis and the nature of the study, under the pretense that they were being treated for "bad blood," a vague term used at the time.

Throughout the study, the researchers observed the devastating effects of untreated syphilis. They documented the primary, secondary, and tertiary phases of the disease, providing extensive data on its progression. However, these findings came at an unacceptable human cost, as many participants suffered serious complications and premature death.

The impact on the participants was catastrophic. In addition to health complications, the study perpetuated distrust of the medical system among the African-American community. Many men died from syphilis, passed the disease on to their wives, and children were born with congenital syphilis.

In 1972, journalist Jean Heller exposed the study in the New York Times, causing public outrage and ending the experiment. The revelation led to a congressional investigation and the implementation of new regulations for the protection of human subjects in research.

In 1973, a class-action lawsuit was filed, resulting in a $10 million settlement for survivors and their families. In addition, the case prompted the creation of the National Commission for the Protection of Human Subjects of Biomedical and Behavioral Research, and the implementation of stricter ethical guidelines, including the requirement for informed consent.

In 1997, President Bill Clinton issued a formal apology on behalf of the United States government, acknowledging the harm caused and the betrayal of the African-American community.

4. The Holmesburg Prison Experiments

Between 1951 and 1974, Holmesburg Prison in Philadelphia, Pennsylvania, was the site of a series of controversial medical experiments conducted on inmates. These studies, led primarily by Dr. Albert Kligman, involved exposure to various chemicals and pharmacological substances without proper informed consent.

Medical research in prisons has been a common practice in the history of medicine, but the experiments conducted at Holmesburg Prison stand out for their lack of ethics and exploitation of a vulnerable population. Between 1951 and 1974, inmates at Holmesburg were subjected to a variety of experiments involving the application of chemicals and pharmacological substances, without being fully informed of the risks and with the promise of minimal financial compensation.

During the 1950s and 1960s, the pharmaceutical industry experienced rapid growth, and the need for clinical trials increased significantly. Prisons, with their captive population, became a convenient resource for these trials. In this context, Holmesburg Prison was used as a human laboratory for testing chemicals and pharmaceuticals.

The main purpose of the experiments was to test the safety and efficacy of various products, including dermatological agents, personal hygiene products, radioactive substances, and industrial chemicals. These studies were funded by pharmaceutical companies, universities, and the United States government.

Participating prisoners were often offered a small financial compensation, which was attractive to the inmates, many of whom came from disadvantaged socioeconomic backgrounds. However, they were not provided with adequate information about the risks and nature of the experiments.

The experiments conducted at Holmesburg included:

Testing of Dermatological Agents: Various chemicals were applied to the skin of inmates to study their effects. These agents included cleaning products, lotions, and creams, many of which caused burns, rashes, and other adverse reactions.

Industrial Chemical Exposure: Inmates were exposed to chemicals such as dioxins and other toxic agents to study their long-term effects on human health.

Radiation Testing: In some cases, inmates were exposed to radioactive substances to observe the effects of radiation on the body.

Pharmaceutical Testing: Experimental drugs were administered to evaluate their safety and effectiveness, often resulting in serious side effects.

The experiments at Holmesburg Prison produced a significant amount of data on the toxicity and effectiveness of various chemicals and pharmaceuticals. This data benefited the companies and institutions that funded the studies but was obtained at a considerable human cost.

Prisoners who participated in the experiments suffered numerous adverse effects, including chemical burns, chronic illness, and in some cases, death. The lack of informed consent and the taking advantage of a vulnerable population were particularly reprehensible aspects of these experiments.

The practice of conducting experiments at Holmesburg Prison began to decline in the 1970s due to growing public awareness and criticism over the ethics of using prisoners as research subjects. In 1974, the experiments were finally suspended.

In 1978, the United States Congress enacted the National Research Act, which established ethical principles for biomedical and behavioral research and created the National Commission for the Protection of Human Subjects of Biomedical and Behavioral Research.

5. Project MKUltra

Project MKUltra was a secret program of the United States Central Intelligence Agency (CIA), carried out from the 1950s to the early 1970s. Its goal was to develop techniques and drugs for mind control, using methods such as the administration of LSD, hypnosis, and sensory deprivation on human subjects.

In the context of the Cold War, Project MKUltra emerged as a CIA response to fears that the Soviet Union and other enemies were developing advanced mind control techniques. This top-secret program involved experimentation on thousands of American and foreign citizens, often without their knowledge or consent, resulting in serious ethical and legal violations.

The CIA was concerned by reports that the Soviet Union, China, and North Korea were using brainwashing techniques to control American prisoners of war. In response, the CIA sought to develop its own mind control techniques.

The main goal of MKUltra was to research and develop methods to control human behavior. This included the use of psychedelic drugs, hypnosis, sensory deprivation, isolation, and other psychological and physical manipulation techniques.

Project MKUltra subjects included prisoners, patients in psychiatric hospitals, drug addicts, and people who were unaware that they were being experimented on. Some experiments were even carried out on ordinary citizens, without their knowledge or consent.

The methods employed in MKUltra were extremely diverse and often brutal. These included:

<u>LSD Administration:</u> The CIA gave subjects LSD to study its effects on behavior and the mind. This was done in controlled environments and sometimes in everyday situations to observe uninduced reactions.

Hypnosis: This was used to explore the possibility of implanting false memories and controlling the behavior of people under hypnotic trance.

Sensory Deprivation: Subjects were subjected to long periods of isolation and sensory deprivation to study the effects on their mental state.

Electroshock and Radiation: Researchers also tested the use of electroshock and radiation as a means of mind control and behavioral alteration.

MKUltra was conducted at numerous universities, hospitals, and research centers throughout the United States and Canada. Dr. Sidney Gottlieb was one of the principal scientists behind the program and is referred to as the CIA's "chief chemist" during this period.

Project MKUltra produced numerous reports and findings, although many of the official documents were destroyed in 1973 by order of then-CIA Director Richard Helms. Despite the destruction of much of the documentation, it is known that the LSD experiments did not produce the expected results and caused psychological harm to numerous patients.

Many of the MKUltra subjects suffered severe adverse effects, including psychosis, brain damage, and in some cases, death. The unethical use of mind control techniques and the lack of informed consent led to lasting damage and widespread distrust of CIA practices.

Project MKUltra was exposed to the public in the 1970s through journalistic investigations and US Congressional hearings. In 1974, the New York Times published an article revealing the existence of secret CIA experimentation programs, leading to a series of official investigations.

In 1975, the US Senate Church Committee conducted an investigation into CIA activities, including MKUltra. This investigation revealed the extent of unethical practices and led to significant reforms in CIA policies and oversight of intelligence activities.

6. Radiation Experiments in Cincinnati

Between 1960 and 1971, a team of researchers at Cincinnati General Hospital conducted a series of radiation experiments on cancer patients. These studies, funded by the United States Department of Defense, were intended to investigate the effects of radiation on cancer treatment and radiation resistance in the context of nuclear war.

During the Cold War, fear of nuclear attack prompted the Department of Defense to explore methods to improve the survival and treatment of people exposed to radiation. The experiments in Cincinnati were framed in this context, with the intention of better understanding the effects of radiation on the human body.

The main goal of the experiments was to investigate the effects of radiation on cancer patients, both to evaluate possible treatments and to understand how radiation might affect soldiers in a nuclear war scenario. The researchers hoped to develop protocols to increase radiation resistance and improve treatment techniques for advanced cancers.

The participants in the experiments were patients with advanced cancer, most of whom were low-income and African-American. Many of them were not fully informed about the nature and risks of the experiments. In several cases, they were told that they were receiving cancer treatments, with no mention of the true purposes of the study.

The experiments involved administering significant doses of radiation to the patients, at levels much higher than those used in standard radiation therapy treatments. The procedures included:

<u>Total Radiation Therapy:</u> Administration of radiation to the entire body to study its systemic effects.

<u>Partial Radiation Therapy:</u> Targeting radiation to specific areas of the body, particularly organs such as the liver and lungs.

Continuous evaluation of the patients was carried out to observe the immediate and long-term effects of radiation exposure.

Cincinnati General Hospital, along with the University of Cincinnati, were the main institutions involved in these experiments. Funding and oversight came largely from the United States Department of Defense.

The experiments provided data on the effects of radiation on the human body, including the response of different organs and systems to radiation damage. However, the results did not lead to significant advances in cancer treatment or in improving radiation resistance for military purposes.

Many of the patients suffered severe adverse effects, including pain, radiation burns, weakened immune systems, and in some cases, death. The high doses of radiation caused considerable suffering, exacerbating patients' pre-existing conditions rather than providing relief or cure.

Details of the radiation experiments in Cincinnati were not made public until the 1990s when reports and testimonies from participants and their families began to attract media and law enforcement attention. In 1994, President Bill Clinton ordered the creation of the Advisory Committee on Human Radiation Experiments to investigate these and similar experiments.

The Advisory Committee published a report in 1995 condemning the practices used in the Cincinnati experiments. This report highlighted the lack of informed consent and ethical violations that had been committed. As a result, new regulations were implemented to protect human subjects in research, including stricter standards for informed consent and ethical oversight.

7. Mustard Gas Experiments on Soldiers

During World War II (1939-1945), the United States conducted a series of experiments using mustard gas on soldiers to study its effects and develop protective and treatment measures in the erman of chemical attacks. These experiments carried out without the informed consent of the participants, represented serious ethical violations and left physical and psychological scars on ermane the soldiers involved.

Mustard gas, also known as mustard gas, had been used during World War I (1914-1918), causing painful and debilitating wounds. Given the possibility of its use in World War II, the United States Department of Defense considered it vital to investigate its effects under controlled conditions.

The main objective of the mustard gas experiments was to understand how the chemical agent affected humans, identify the best treatments for chemical burns, and develop effective protective clothing and equipment. The aim was also to study the resistance of soldiers to different concentrations and conditions of exposure.

The participants in these experiments were volunteer soldiers who in many cases were not fully informed about the risks. They were often told that the tests were of "great importance to national security" and could help erm lives on the battlefield. Manipulation of information and deception about the nature of the experiments were prominent features of these tests.

Experimental Procedures:

<u>Direct Exposure:</u> Soldiers were exposed to mustard gas in sealed gas chambers, where the immediate and subsequent effects on their skin and respiratory systems were observed.

<u>Field Tests:</u> In some cases, experiments were conducted in open field conditions, where soldiers performed physical exercises under mustard gas exposure to simulate combat conditions.

<u>Skin Application:</u> In other experiments, small amounts of liquid mustard gas were applied directly to soldiers' skin to study skin reactions and develop treatments for chemical burns.

<u>Equipment and Protection:</u> The experiments also included testing different types of clothing and protective masks to assess their effectiveness against mustard gas.

The experiments were primarily conducted by the U.S. Army at facilities such as the Edgewood Chemical Test Range and Camp Sibert Military Training Range in Alabama. Other laboratories and research centers were also involved in these tests.

The experiments provided valuable information about the effects of mustard gas on the human body, including chemical burns, respiratory damage, and systemic effects. Progress was also made in the development of protective equipment and medical treatments for victims of chemical attacks. However, these scientific findings came at the   ermane soldiers' suffering.

ermane the soldiers exposed to mustard gas suffered severe burns, ermanente scarring, and chronic respiratory problems. In addition to physical damage, many experienced psychological trauma due to the painful and dangerous nature of the experiments. The lack of informed consent and the exploitation of soldiers' trust represented significant ethical violations.

Most details about the mustard gas experiments remained classified for decades. It wasn't until the 1990s that documents began to be declassified, and the stories of veterans who participated in these experiments came to light. The revelations sparked public outrage and led to additional investigations.

As details of the experiments became known, there were calls for accountability and compensation for affected veterans. In 1991, the U.S. Congress passed the Chemical Warfare Veterans Compensation Act, which provided benefits to veterans who participated in experiments involving mustard gas and other chemical agents.

8. Project 4.1

Project 4.1 was developed against a backdrop of intensified nuclear testing during the Cold War. The "Castle Bravo" test, conducted on March 1, 1954, was the most powerful detonation carried out by the United States at Bikini Atoll, Marshall Islands. The explosion exceeded expectations in terms of power and radiation release, affecting local residents and crew members of nearby fishing boats. Project 4.1 was conceived to study the effects of this radiation exposure on humans.

In the 1950s, in the context of the Cold War, the United States and the Soviet Union were engaged in a nuclear arms race. The Marshall Islands, under American administration after World War II, became a key site for nuclear testing. The "Castle Bravo" test was part of Operation Castle, a series of hydrogen bomb tests.

The stated goal of Project 4.1 was to study the medical and biological effects of radiation exposure on island residents near the nuclear test site. Researchers sought to obtain data that could help better understand the effects of radiation on human health, in order to improve medical responses in the event of a nuclear war.

The subjects of Project 4.1 were primarily residents of Rongelap Atoll and Utirik Atoll, who were exposed to high levels of radiation following the "Castle Bravo" test. Approximately 82 residents of Rongelap and 157 residents of Utirik were tested. Selection was not voluntary and participants were not fully notified of the nature and risks of the study.

Experimental Procedures:

<u>Initial Medical Evaluations:</u> Immediately following the test, residents were evacuated and subjected to medical examinations to assess the immediate effects of radiation. These examinations included blood tests, skin biopsies, and monitoring for acute symptoms such as burns and nausea.

<u>Long-Term Follow-Up:</u> Studies continued for decades, with periodic assessments to monitor long-term effects such as cancer, thyroid disease, and other chronic health problems.

<u>Biological Data Collection:</u> Researchers collected blood, urine, and tissue samples for detailed analysis of radiation effects on biological systems.

Project 4.1 was conducted primarily by the U.S. Department of Defense and the Atomic Energy Commission (AEC). Medical and research institutions, including the University of California and Brookhaven National Laboratory, also participated.

Initial and follow-up studies revealed that radiation exposure caused a range of adverse health effects, including:

<u>Acute radiation symptoms:</u> Skin burns, hair loss, nausea, and vomiting.

<u>Thyroid Disease:</u> Elevated incidence of hypothyroidism and thyroid cancer due to exposure to radioactive iodine.

<u>Cancer:</u> Increased incidence of several types of cancer, including leukemia and skin cancer.

<u>Genetic effects:</u> Potential risks of birth defects and other abnormalities in future generations.

Marshallese residents suffered significantly from their exposure to radiation. Many developed serious, chronic illnesses, and cancer mortality was markedly increased. Forced displacement and the loss of their traditional homes also had a profound impact on the culture and well-being of the affected communities.

Project 4.1 and its details were not immediately made public. It was in the 1980s and 1990s that information began to come to light, driven by demands for transparency and justice by Marshallese residents and human rights activists.

The revelation of Project 4.1 led to significant criticism and a re-evaluation of ethical standards in research. In 1986, the United States signed the Compact of Free Association with the Marshall Islands, which included compensation and the establishment of the Marshall Islands Health Program to provide ongoing medical care for people affected by nuclear testing.

9. Yale Prefrontal Cortex Experiments

The 1960s were a period of great advancement in the field of neuroscience, with scientists exploring new frontiers in understanding the human brain. In this context, the experiments conducted by Dr. José Delgado at Yale University were notable for their boldness and for the ethical questions they raised about manipulating human behavior through brain stimulation.

The 1960s witnessed a growing interest in brain functions and how manipulating certain areas of the brain could influence behavior. The prefrontal cortex, known for its role in executive functions, decision-making, and controlling social behavior, became a focus of research.

The main goal of Delgado's experiments was to understand how electrical stimulation of the prefrontal cortex could alter human behavior and emotions. In the long term, he hoped that these studies could lead to new ways of treating mental illness and controlling deviant behavior.

The participants in these studies included both animals (primarily primates) and humans. In the case of humans, the participants were mostly psychiatric patients who had given consent, although the level of information provided and the nature of the consent have been the subject of debate.

Experimental Procedures:

<u>Electrode Implantation:</u> Delgado developed devices known as "brain stimulators" that were implanted in the prefrontal cortex. These electrodes could be remotely controlled to stimulate specific areas of the brain.

<u>Controlled Stimulation:</u> The experiments involved applying electrical currents through the implanted electrodes to observe changes in behavior, emotions, and physiological responses.

<u>Observation and Recording:</u> Changes in the subjects were meticulously recorded, including alterations in mood, aggression, docility, and other behavioral responses.

The experiments were conducted in the Department of Neurophysiology at Yale University, under the direct supervision of Dr. José Delgado and his team of researchers.

Delgado's experiments provided several insights into the functioning of the prefrontal cortex and its influence on behavior:

<u>Behavioral Modulation:</u> Stimulating certain areas of the prefrontal cortex was able to induce significant changes in behavior, such as reducing aggression or inducing states of euphoria.

<u>Remote Behavior Control:</u> The experiments demonstrated the possibility of controlling subjects' behavior through electrical stimulation, opening

debates about the applications and ethical implications of this technology.

<u>Potential Therapeutic Applications:</u> It was suggested that these techniques could have applications in the treatment of psychiatric disorders, although risks and limitations were evident.

The experiments had varied impacts on human participants, from temporary improvements in mood to adverse effects such as anxiety and dysphoria. The primates used in the studies showed significant behavioral changes, although these also raised ethical questions about animal welfare.

The details of these experiments were published in several scientific papers during the 1960s, attracting both praise for their innovations and criticism for their ethical implications. Over time, ethical scrutiny and changes in research regulations led to a decline in such invasive studies.

Delgado's experiments raised important ethical questions about the manipulation of human behavior. Concerns included the possibility of abuse of technology for social control and the lack of fully informed consent from participants. These studies contributed to the evolution of ethical regulations in research, emphasizing the need to protect the rights and well-being of human subjects.

10. The Willowbrook Study

The Willowbrook Study was conducted against a backdrop of growing interest in medical research into infectious diseases and the search for effective treatments. However, the study has been widely criticized for its ethical practices and its impact on the participants, who were children with intellectual disabilities living in a state institution.

The Willowbrook State Institution, located on Staten Island, New York, and established in 1947, was a home for children with intellectual disabilities. During the 1950s and 1960s, hepatitis was a growing concern in the medical field, with recurring outbreaks at similar institutions. In response, the Willowbrook Study was designed to investigate hepatitis and develop a vaccine, but its methods soon became the center of controversy.

The primary goal of the Willowbrook Study was to study the course and prevention of viral hepatitis, particularly hepatitis A and B. The goal was to understand how the disease spread in institutional settings and to evaluate the effectiveness of an experimental vaccine.

Study participants were children with intellectual disabilities residing at Willowbrook. Often, the families of these children were not fully informed about the nature of the studies and the level of risk involved. Selection was not completely voluntary, and options for declining participation were limited.

Experimental Procedures:

<u>Intentional Infection:</u> One of the most controversial aspects of the study was the intentional inoculation of children with hepatitis to observe disease progression and test the efficacy of an experimental vaccine. Researchers injected children with hepatitis viruses and observed the development of the disease.

<u>Observation and Monitoring:</u> Children were closely monitored to document symptoms, disease progression, and responses to the vaccine. Regular examinations were performed and samples were collected for analysis.

<u>Treatment and Vaccination:</u> In addition to inoculation, the study included attempts at treatment and vaccination to evaluate their efficacy in preventing and controlling hepatitis.

The study was led by Dr. Saul Krugman and his team at the Willowbrook facility, in collaboration with several medical institutions and universities, including New York University and New York University Hospital.

The Willowbrook Study provided insight into the spread and treatment of hepatitis in institutional settings:

<u>Transmission Patterns:</u> Researchers confirmed that hepatitis A and B were easily spread in settings with high population density and poor living conditions.

<u>Vaccine Development:</u> The study contributed to the development of an effective hepatitis A vaccine, which

later became an important resource for disease prevention.

<u>Hepatitis Characteristics:</u> The clinical features of hepatitis were documented in a vulnerable population, helping to improve knowledge about the disease.

The children involved in the study suffered the direct consequences of infection and complications associated with hepatitis. Many experienced serious adverse effects, including prolonged illness, liver complications, and physical suffering. The study's practices raised significant concerns about the well-being and rights of participants.

In the 1970s, the Willowbrook Study was the subject of journalistic investigations and public scrutiny. In particular, journalist Geraldo Rivera exposed the inhumane conditions at the Willowbrook Institution in his 1972 television report, leading to heightened public awareness and the eventual discontinuation of the study.

The Willowbrook Study sparked intense debate about ethics in medical research and the treatment of people with disabilities. The revelations led to a re-evaluation of standards for informed consent and the protection of research subjects.

11. AIDS Experiments on Orphaned Children

In the 1980s, HIV/AIDS had become a global epidemic, and efforts to find effective treatments were intense. In New York, as in many other cities, medical centers and research institutions faced the challenge of developing therapies for a disease that was still poorly understood. Among the studies conducted, some involved orphaned children living in care institutions.

The main objective of these experiments was to evaluate the efficacy and safety of experimental treatments for HIV/AIDS in a child population. The studies sought to understand how the treatments influenced the progression of the disease and its side effects in a group of patients with specific characteristics.

The participants in these studies were primarily orphaned children residing in care institutions in New York. These children, often in poor health conditions due to their situation, were selected for the experiments because of their high vulnerability to HIV/AIDS. Recruiting participants and obtaining consent were problematic, as many of the children were in institutions and their biological families were not present to provide adequate informed consent.

Experimental Treatments: The studies involved the administration of experimental HIV/AIDS medications and therapies. These treatments were in the trial phase and were not approved for general use.

<u>Monitoring and Evaluation:</u> The children were closely monitored to assess treatment efficacy and side effects. Regular medical examinations were performed, and blood and other body fluid samples were collected.

<u>Documentation and Reporting:</u> Data on disease progression and response to treatments were carefully documented. These reports were used to assess the impact of the treatments and adjust protocols.

The experiments were conducted at several institutions and hospitals in New York, including New York Children's Hospital, Bellevue Hospital, and other research centers specializing in infectious diseases and pediatrics.

Some of the treatments tested showed promise in reducing viral load and improving patients' overall health.

The studies also revealed a range of side effects associated with the treatments, including serious adverse reactions and long-term tolerance problems.

The data helped to understand how HIV/AIDS progressed in children and how experimental therapies could modify that progression.

The impact on orphaned children was significant. Many of the participants experienced serious adverse effects from the experimental treatments. The lack of informed consent and the vulnerability of the children raised serious ethical and human rights issues.

The controversial nature of these studies became more apparent as the research practices became known. Public criticism and reports from activists and journalists led to a review of research methods and increased pressure to improve ethical practices.

12. Electroshock Experiments on Children

During the 1940s to 1960s, electroshock treatment (or electroconvulsive therapy, ECT) was widely used in children to treat various psychiatric conditions. Although this practice was promoted by some as a therapeutic breakthrough, it is today considered one of the most controversial practices in the history of child psychiatry.

ECT was introduced in the 1930s by Italian psychiatrists Ugo Cerletti and Lucio Bini. In its early days, ECT was primarily used on adults to treat schizophrenia and severe depression. However, during the 1940s and 1950s, some psychiatrists began applying this technique to children who had psychiatric disorders, under the premise that it could be equally beneficial for this younger population.

The main goal of applying ECT to children was to treat psychiatric conditions such as schizophrenia, autism, severe depression, and other serious behavioral disorders. Doctors hoped that ECT could reduce severe symptoms and improve the quality of life of these children.

The children who underwent ECT were usually patients in psychiatric hospitals or institutions for children with mental disabilities. Many of these children came from vulnerable backgrounds, and in many cases, parents or legal guardians gave consent under pressure from doctors, who claimed that ECT was an effective treatment.

Experimental Procedures:

<u>Application of Electric Shocks:</u> ECT involves the application of electric currents through the brain to induce seizures. In children, sessions varied in frequency and intensity, tailored according to the patient's response.

<u>Monitoring Responses:</u> Doctors observed the children's physical and emotional responses during and after the ECT sessions. Side effects were common and included confusion, memory loss, and behavioral changes.

<u>Documentation of Outcomes:</u> Outcomes and observations were meticulously documented. However, the lack of ethical standards and long-term follow-up makes these records questionable in terms of their rigor and objectivity.

Electroshock experiments on children were conducted at a variety of psychiatric institutions and hospitals in the United States and Europe. Notable among these institutions were Bellevue State Hospital in New York and several psychiatric hospitals in the United Kingdom.

The scientific findings of these studies were mixed and often contradictory:

Temporary Improvements: In some cases, physicians reported temporary improvements in children's psychiatric symptoms, such as a reduction in aggression or improvement in mood.

Adverse Side Effects: Negative side effects were common and often severe. Children experience memory loss, confusion, and in some cases, worsening of psychiatric symptoms.

Lack of Long-Term Evidence: The lack of long-term studies and the absence of adequate follow-up limit the validity of the reported positive results.

The impact of ECT on children was significant and, in many cases, detrimental. Short-term effects included confusion, headache, and behavioral changes. In the long term, some children experience cognitive and emotional impairment. The experience of undergoing ECT also had a profound psychological impact on many children.

As knowledge about the effects of ECT advanced and awareness of patient rights increased, the use of electroshock in children began to be seriously questioned. In the 1960s and 1970s, growing criticism and advances in pharmacotherapy led to a significant decline in the use of ECT in child psychiatry.

13. Forced Sterilization Program in the United States

Between 1907 and 1979, the United States implemented a forced sterilization program targeting people deemed "unfit" to reproduce. This program, based on the principles of eugenics, sought to improve the genetic quality of the population. Forced sterilization practices affected tens of thousands of people, including racial minorities, people with disabilities, and other vulnerable groups.

The eugenics movement in the United States emerged in the late 19th and early 20th centuries, influenced by the theories of genetic enhancement and natural selection. Prominent scientists and social leaders promoted the idea that humanity could be improved by limiting the reproduction of those considered "weak" or "defective."

Indiana was the first state to pass a sterilization law in 1907. The law allowed for the sterilization of people in mental institutions and penitentiaries. Soon, other states followed suit, and by the 1930s, more than 30 states had passed similar laws.

Individuals targeted for forced sterilization included those in institutions for the mentally and physically handicapped, prisoners, and in many cases, poor and ethnic minority individuals. Criteria for sterilization varied by state and institution, but commonly included diagnoses of "imbecility," "idiocy," "insanity," "criminality," and "feeblemindedness."

Forced sterilization was performed through surgical procedures such as tubal ligation in women and vasectomy in men. These procedures were performed without the informed consent of the subjects, and often without their prior knowledge.

Sterilizations were carried out in a variety of institutions, including mental hospitals, reformatories, prisons, and public hospitals. Physicians and administrators at these institutions played a key role in identifying and carrying out sterilizations.

It is estimated that around 60,000 to 70,000 people were forcibly sterilized in the United States during the program. California, North Carolina, and Virginia were some of the states with the highest numbers of sterilizations.

Victims of forced sterilization suffered not only the loss of their reproductive capacity but also significant psychological trauma. Many faced social stigmatization, and their human rights and dignity were severely violated.

The forced sterilization program reflected and reinforced discriminatory and racist attitudes in American society. The most affected groups included ethnic minorities, such as African Americans, Latinos, and Native Americans, as well as people with disabilities and mental health issues.

Beginning in the 1960s, the civil rights movement and growing awareness of human rights began to question and oppose forced sterilization practices. Changes in legislation and public policy, as well as increased protection of individual rights, led to the decline and eventual termination of the program.

The most prominent court case involving forced sterilization is Buck v. Bell (1927), in which the U.S. Supreme Court upheld the constitutionality of forced sterilization laws. The Court's decision, written by Justice Oliver Wendell Holmes Jr., infamously stated, "Three generations of imbeciles are enough." This ruling legitimized the practice for decades.

In recent decades, some states have officially acknowledged the injustices committed during the forced sterilization program. States such as Virginia, North Carolina, and California have issued official apologies and established compensation programs for surviving victims.

14. Sleep Deprivation Experiments

During the 1960s, sleep deprivation experiments were widely conducted to understand the effects of sleep on mental and physical health. These studies, conducted at various research institutions, sought to explore how sleep deprivation affected subjects' behavior, cognitive performance, and overall well-being.

The mid-20th century saw intense scientific and medical research. Advances in technology and methodology allowed researchers to study sleep more precisely. Sleep deprivation, in particular, became an area of interest due to its potential implications on human performance, mental health, and physiology.

The main goals of sleep deprivation experiments were to:

Understand physiological effects: Examine how sleep deprivation affects the body, including the cardiovascular, immune, and endocrine systems.

Evaluate cognitive impact: Study how sleep deprivation influences cognitive functions such as memory, attention, decision-making, and reaction time.

Explore psychological consequences: Analyze the effects of sleep deprivation on mood, behavior, and mental health.

Participants in these studies were generally volunteers, including college students and military personnel. Young, healthy people were often selected to minimize the risks associated with sleep deprivation.

Experimental Procedures:

Total Sleep Deprivation: In some experiments, subjects were kept awake for extended periods, ranging from 24 hours to several consecutive days.

Partial Sleep Deprivation: Other studies limited the amount of sleep subjects could get each night, reducing it to a few hours over an extended period.

Monitoring and Evaluation: During the experiments, subjects were continuously monitored to assess their physiological, cognitive, and emotional responses. A variety of methods were used, including neuropsychological testing, electroencephalograms (EEGs), and behavioral observations.

These experiments were conducted at a variety of academic and military institutions. Among the most notable were renowned universities and military research centers seeking to better understand how sleep deprivation affected soldiers' performance.

Scientific Findings:

Physiological Effects: Sleep deprivation resulted in a number of physiological changes, including increases in blood pressure, and heart rate, and elevated levels of stress hormones such as cortisol.

Cognitive Impact: Studies showed that sleep deprivation significantly impaired cognitive functions. Subjects showed decreased attention, reaction time, and decision-making ability, as well as short-term memory problems.

Psychological Consequences: Sleep deprivation had a negative impact on mood and behavior. Subjects experienced irritability, anxiety, depression, and in extreme cases, hallucinations and delusions.

The effects of sleep deprivation on participants were profound. In the short term, subjects experienced extreme fatigue, disorientation, and impaired performance. In the long term, some studies suggested that chronic sleep deprivation could have lasting effects on mental and physical health.

One of the major ethical controversies of these experiments was the issue of informed consent. In some cases, participants were not fully informed about the potential risks of sleep deprivation, raising serious ethical concerns about their well-being.

The risks associated with the absence of a good night's sleep are significant. Lack of sleep can lead to severe cognitive impairment, cardiovascular problems, and mental disorders. Exposure of participants to these risks without adequate mitigation measures was another point of criticism.

Participants' well-being was often compromised in these studies. The negative effects of sleep deprivation, both short- and long-term, raised questions about the ethics of subjecting subjects to such extreme conditions.

As sleep science advanced, researchers began to recognize the risks and ethical limitations of these experiments. Later studies were conducted with greater emphasis on ethics and informed consent, and less invasive methods of studying sleep were developed.

Despite the controversies, the sleep deprivation experiments of the 1960s made significant contributions to the scientific understanding of sleep. These studies helped establish its importance for mental and physical health and fostered the development of sleep neuroscience as a legitimate field of study.

15. The Study of Down Syndrome in Institutions

Down syndrome, a genetic condition caused by the presence of an extra copy of chromosome 21, has been the subject of scientific study for many decades. During the 1960s and 1970s, several studies focused on people with Down syndrome living in institutions. These studies aimed to better understand the medical, psychological, and social characteristics of the syndrome but also raised ethical controversies due to the treatment of participants and the conditions under which they were conducted.

For much of the 20th century, people with intellectual disabilities, including those with Down syndrome, were often institutionalized. Institutions were seen as places where these people could receive care and protection. However, conditions in many of these facilities were deplorable, and residents often suffered abuse and neglect.

In the decades noted above, scientific interest in Down syndrome grew significantly. Advances in genetics and medicine prompted studies aimed at better understanding the biology and development of people with this condition. Institutions, where large groups of people with Down syndrome lived, became convenient locations to conduct this research. Often, these studies included children and young adults who had been institutionalized from an early age.

The studies varied widely in their approach and methodology but commonly included:

Medical Evaluations: Detailed physical examinations to document the medical and physical characteristics associated with Down syndrome.

Psychological Testing: Cognitive and behavioral assessments to understand the intellectual and emotional development of participants.

Genetic Studies: Chromosomal and genetic analyses to investigate the causes and characteristics of Down syndrome.

Numerous institutions in the United States and Europe participated in these studies. Among the most prominent were large psychiatric institutions and research centers at universities.

The studies helped identify many of the physical and medical characteristics associated with Down syndrome, such as a predisposition to congenital heart disease, gastrointestinal problems, and endocrine conditions.

Psychological evaluations showed wide variability in the intellectual development and adaptive skills of people with Down syndrome, challenging the idea that all people with the condition have similar levels of disability.

In turn, genetic studies confirmed that Down syndrome is caused by a trisomy of chromosome 21, leading to a better understanding of the biology of the condition.

While the studies provided valuable information, participants often suffered due to living conditions in institutions and a lack of adequate informed consent. Medical and psychological evaluations were sometimes invasive and stressful, and research results rarely directly benefited participants.

A major ethical concern was the lack of informed consent. Many participants were unable to fully understand the nature and risks of the studies because of their intellectual disabilities, and in many cases, consents were granted by institutional administrators without due consideration of the rights of the individuals.

Conditions in many institutions were inadequate and often inhumane. Residents suffered from overcrowding, poor hygiene, and substandard medical care. Research in these settings raised serious ethical questions about the treatment of study subjects.

The results of the studies were often used to advance academic and scientific careers, with no clear benefit to the participants. The dehumanization of people with Down syndrome as mere objects of study was a frequent criticism.

Beginning in the 1970s, the disability rights movement began to gain momentum. Growing criticism of institutional conditions and the treatment of people with disabilities led to significant reforms in policy and practice.

Ethical standards in research became stricter, with greater emphasis on informed consent and protection of participants' rights. Research began to focus more on the inclusion and participation of people with disabilities in society.

Despite controversies, studies from the 1960s and 1970s provided valuable information that helped improve the understanding and treatment of Down syndrome. Findings about the medical characteristics, cognitive development, and genetics of the condition remain relevant today.

16. The Stanford Prison Experiments

The Stanford Prison Experiment, conducted in 1971 by psychologist Philip Zimbardo, is one of the most well-known and controversial studies in the history of social psychology. This experiment, which aimed to investigate the psychological effects of (fictional) imprisonment, quickly became an example of how circumstances and roles can influence human behavior.

Over the course of six days, the experiment demonstrated how individuals can engage in extreme behavior when placed in an environment of power and submission. While the study provided valuable insights into the psychology of power and authority, it also raised profound ethical questions about the researcher's responsibility and the well-being of the participants.

In the 1960s and early 1970s, social psychology was increasingly interested in how social roles and situations influenced human behavior. Studies such as Stanley Milgram's 1963 obedience study demonstrated how authority can lead people to act against their moral principles.

Philip Zimbardo, a psychologist at Stanford University, wanted to further explore how extreme situations can change human behavior. Inspired by prison riots and the growing interest in the psychology of incarceration, Zimbardo designed an experiment to simulate prison conditions and observe how participants behaved when they were assigned the roles of either guards or prisoners.

The experiment recruited 24 male college students through newspaper advertisements, offering them compensation for participating. Participants were selected for their psychological and physical stability and were randomly divided into two groups: guards and prisoners.

The basement of Stanford's psychology building was converted into a mock prison. Cells were built, and areas for guards and observation spaces were set up. Prisoners were arrested by real police officers (in collaboration with the university) at their homes without warning and taken to the mock prison, where they were subjected to an intake procedure that included being stripped of their clothes, disinfected, and dressed in prisoner uniforms.

Roles and Procedures:

<u>Guards:</u> Guards were given uniforms, reflective sunglasses, and batons, and instructed to maintain order without using physical violence. They were given considerable authority over the prisoners and encouraged to develop their own procedures for maintaining control.

<u>Prisoners:</u> Prisoners were assigned to cells and given numbers rather than names. They were subjected to strict rules and a daily regimen monitored by the guards.

The experiment was scheduled to last two weeks, with ongoing observations and video recordings to document participants' behavior.

The experiment, which was supposed to last two weeks, was interrupted after just six days due to extreme behavior that emerged:

<u>Guards:</u> Some guards began to display sadistic and abusive behavior. They implemented arbitrary punishments, humiliated prisoners, and exercised their power in oppressive ways.

<u>Prisoners:</u> Prisoners began to show signs of severe stress, anxiety, and despair. Some rebelled, while others passively submitted to the abuses.

The experiment showed how ordinary people can adopt extreme behaviors under certain circumstances. The rapid adoption of roles and depersonalization of prisoners and guards highlighted the influence of social context and power structures on human behavior.

Although participants gave their consent to take part, many critics argue that they were not fully aware of the nature and potential risks of the experiment. The lack of preparation for the psychological extremes they experienced raises serious ethical concerns.

Philip Zimbardo, who acted as superintendent of the simulated prison, failed to adequately intervene when guards began to abuse their power. The lack of early intervention to protect the well-being of participants was a point of significant criticism.

The negative psychological impact on participants was considerable. Some prisoners experienced emotional breakdowns and severe stress, leading to early termination of the experiment. The conditions created in the study were considered inhumane by many critics.

The experiment was stopped after six days, largely due to the intervention of Christina Maslach, a colleague of Zimbardo, who raised concerns about the ethics and well-being of participants. Her reaction helped Zimbardo recognize the seriousness of the situation and end the study prematurely.

The experiment received considerable attention from the media and the academic community. While some praised the findings for providing deep insight into human behavior under stress, others harshly criticized the study's methods and ethics.

The Stanford Prison Experiment has been pivotal in understanding the psychology of social roles and power. The findings have been applied in studies of abuse of power, behavior in institutions, and crisis situations.

The experiment's ethical controversy has led to increased regulation and oversight of psychological research. Stricter standards have been put in place regarding informed consent, researcher intervention, and protection of participant welfare.

The experiment has inspired numerous books, documentaries, and films, and remains a reference point in debates about ethics in research and the nature of human behavior.

17. The Chicago Prisoner Malaria Studies

In the 1940s, malaria studies in prisoners at the Illinois State Prison in Chicago represented a significant effort to combat malaria during World War II. These studies, conducted under the supervision of Dr. Alf Alving and other researchers, involved deliberately infecting prisoners with malaria to test the efficacy of new treatments. While the studies provided valuable medical data, they also raised serious ethical questions about the consent and treatment of participants.

Malaria is a potentially fatal disease transmitted by mosquitoes. During World War II, malaria caused more casualties among Allied troops in the Pacific than enemy bullets. The urgent need for effective treatments led the United States to invest in accelerated research on the disease.

The Illinois State Prison in Chicago was chosen as the site for the malaria studies because of the availability of a captive population of prisoners, considered suitable to participate in medical research. At the time, the ethics of human research were not as developed as they are today, and it was considered acceptable to conduct studies on prisoners under certain conditions.

Prisoners were recruited for the studies through incentives such as reduced sentences, monetary payments, and improved living conditions during the study. Although they were informed of the risks, the level of informed consent that was obtained is questionable by modern standards.

Experimental Procedures:

<u>Deliberate Infection:</u> Prisoners were deliberately infected with malaria through bites from infected mosquitoes or by injection of malaria parasites.

<u>Administration of Treatments:</u> Various antimalarial drugs were tested, including quinine, atabrine, and other experimental substances. Researchers monitored the effectiveness of these treatments in reducing fever and eliminating the parasite from the body.

Observation and Recording: Participants were closely observed and their symptoms and reactions were carefully documented. Side effects of the treatments were also recorded.

The studies helped identify more effective treatments for malaria, including the use of atabrine, which was found to be more effective and less toxic than quinine. These findings had a direct impact on the management of malaria among Allied troops, saving numerous lives.

The prisoners who participated in the studies experienced varying degrees of illness from malaria and the side effects of the treatments. Some suffered serious complications, while others recovered without lasting problems.

The level of informed consent is one of the most criticized aspects of these studies. Although the prisoners signed consent documents, it is questioned whether they fully understood the risks and nature of the experiment. The circumstances of coercion inherent to their status as prisoners also call into question the voluntariness of their participation.

The use of a captive and vulnerable population for medical experiments raises serious ethical concerns. Prisoners, being in a position of unequal power, may have felt pressure to participate, compromising the validity of their consent.

Although the studies resulted in important medical advances, the balance between societal benefit and individual risk is a central issue in research ethics. The exploitation of prisoners for the benefit of public health raises ethical dilemmas about justice and equality.

Details of the malaria studies in prisoners became more widely publicized in the decades following World War II. Awareness of the ethical aspects of these studies grew as stricter standards for research on humans were developed.

18. The Acid Exposure Experiments in the US

The acid exposure experiments in the 1960s are an example of how scientific research, driven by military needs and technological advances, can cross significant ethical lines.

During the Cold War, research into the effects of and protection against chemical weapons became a priority for the US military. Corrosive acids, used in various military and industrial applications, require extensive study to understand their effects on the human body and develop effective countermeasures.

A number of institutions, including military laboratories, universities, and hospitals, were involved in these studies. Among the best-known were the US Army and several renowned universities that collaborated on research into hazardous chemicals.

Participants in these experiments included military volunteers, prisoners, and occasionally civilians recruited through advertisements. The information provided to participants about the risks involved varied, and in many cases, the level of informed consent was insufficient by today's standards.

Experimental Procedures:

Acid Exposure: Subjects were exposed to different types of acids, such as sulfuric acid and hydrochloric acid, in varying concentrations. Exposure was via controlled topical applications to the skin or, in some cases, inhalation of acid vapors.

Reaction Monitoring: Researchers observed and documented subjects' immediate and long-term reactions, including burns, pain, tissue damage, and systemic effects.

Evaluation and Treatment: The effects of different treatments and countermeasures to mitigate the damage caused by acid exposure were evaluated. This included the use of neutralizing solutions, bandages, and other medical methods.

Results were carefully documented, and the data collected was used to improve safety measures in military and industrial settings. Reports of these studies were often kept classified or disseminated in limited scientific circles.

The experiments revealed a variety of adverse effects of acid exposure, which varied by type of acid, concentration, and duration of exposure. Observed effects included:

• Chemical burns of varying degrees
• Tissue necrosis
• Extreme pain and neurological damage
• Systemic complications in cases of inhalation
• Development of Countermeasures

The studies helped develop effective countermeasures to acid exposure, including specific neutralizing solutions and treatment protocols to minimize damage and speed recovery. These advances were applied in military and industrial settings to improve safety and response to chemical incidents.

Many participants were not fully informed about the risks and nature of the experiments. In some cases, subjects were induced to participate under pressures or incentives that compromised the voluntariness of their consent.

The use of prisoners and military volunteers, who were often in positions of unequal power, raised serious ethical concerns. The ability of these individuals to refuse to participate or fully understand the risks was limited, compromising the ethics of the studies.

While the studies provided valuable information for military and industrial security, the assessment of risks to individuals versus potential benefits to society is a central issue in research ethics. The exploitation of human subjects for medical data raises ethical dilemmas about fairness and humane treatment.

Details of the acid exposure experiments became more widely known in the decades after they were conducted. Public awareness of the ethical aspects of these studies grew as stricter standards for human research were developed.

19. Radiation Studies in Brooklyn Hospitals

During the 1940s, several radiation studies were conducted in hospitals in Brooklyn, New York. These studies, conducted primarily on terminally or chronically ill patients, involved deliberate exposure to doses of radiation with the goal of better understanding its effects on the human body and developing medical treatments and industrial applications.

Radiation was discovered in the late 19th century and its medical and scientific applications were quickly explored. During the 1930s and 1940s, radiation was used both for cancer treatment and for various scientific studies, often without a full understanding of its long-term effects.

In Brooklyn, several hospitals participated in these studies, including institutions such as Brooklyn Jewish Hospital and Kings County Hospital. These institutions became research centers where the effects of radiation on the human body were explored.

The studies often involved terminally or chronically ill patients who received treatment at these hospitals.

Participants were selected based on their health status, and many were not fully informed about the experimental nature of the treatments they received.

Experimental Procedures:

Radiation Exposure: Patients were exposed to various doses of radiation, ranging from low to extremely high. Exposure was via X-rays, radon, and other radioactive isotopes.

Monitoring Reactions: Researchers observed and documented patients' immediate and long-term reactions, including effects on the skin, internal organs, and general health.

Evaluation of Therapeutic Effects: In addition to adverse effects, the studies also evaluated the effectiveness of radiation in treating certain medical conditions, such as cancer.

The results were carefully documented, and the data collected was used to improve medical knowledge about the effects of radiation and to develop more effective treatments.

The studies revealed a variety of adverse effects of radiation exposure, including:

• Burns and tissue damage
• Cardiovascular problems
• Effects on the central nervous system
• Increased risk of cancer and other long-term diseases

Despite the adverse effects, the studies also showed that radiation could be effective in treating certain types of cancer and other diseases, leading to the development of new radiological therapies.

Many patients were not fully informed about the risks and the experimental nature of the treatments. The information provided to patients was often insufficient, compromising the ethics of the studies.

The use of terminally ill or chronically ill patients, who were often in vulnerable and desperate positions, raised serious ethical concerns. The ability of these individuals to fully understand the risks and refuse to participate was limited.

While the studies provided valuable information for medicine, the assessment of the risks to individuals compared to the potential benefits to society is a central issue in research ethics. The exploitation of patients for medical data raises ethical dilemmas about justice and humane treatment.

Details of the radiation studies at Brooklyn hospitals became more widely known in subsequent decades. Public awareness of the ethical aspects of these studies grew as stricter standards for human research were developed.

Despite the controversies, the studies provided crucial data that helped improve medical knowledge and the treatment of diseases using radiation. These advances have had a lasting impact on modern medicine.

20. Chemical Weapons Testing in Vietnamese Villages

During the 1960s, in the context of the Vietnam War, the United States military conducted chemical weapons testing in Vietnamese villages. These tests, which involved the use of chemical agents such as Agent Orange, were conducted with the aim of defoliating forests and eliminating crops used by the Viet Cong. However, the consequences for the civilian population were devastating, causing severe illness and long-term environmental damage.

The Vietnam War (1955–1975) was a protracted conflict between communist forces in North Vietnam and the government of South Vietnam, backed by the United States and other anti-communist nations. The war was characterized by guerrilla tactics, leading the American military to seek unconventional methods to counter the Viet Cong insurgency.

In an attempt to deprive the Viet Cong of vegetation cover and agricultural resources, the United States initiated the program known as "Operation Ranch Hand" in 1961. This program involved spraying herbicides and defoliants, including Agent Orange, over vast areas of jungle and agricultural land in South Vietnam.

The areas selected for chemical weapons testing included villages and rural regions where the Viet Cong were suspected of having a significant presence. The operations were carried out without advance notification to local inhabitants, exposing them directly to the chemicals.

Spraying Procedures:

<u>Use of Aircraft:</u> Herbicides and defoliants were dispersed primarily by C-123 aircraft flying over the designated areas. Spraying missions were conducted regularly throughout the 1960s.

<u>Types of Chemicals:</u> Chemicals used included Agent Orange, which contained dioxins, highly toxic compounds that persist in the environment and cause serious health problems.

<u>Military Objectives:</u> The primary military justification was the removal of vegetation cover and the destruction of crops that could sustain the enemy.

The effects of the spraying were documented through aerial photographs and field reports, which recorded the effectiveness of the chemicals in defoliating and destroying crops.

Herbicides and defoliants devastated the Vietnamese landscape, causing the loss of large areas of forest and agricultural land. The persistence of dioxins in soil and water caused long-term ecological damage.

Local populations exposed to the chemicals suffered a wide range of health problems, including:

• Cancer
• Birth defects
• Skin diseases

• Respiratory and immune system problems
• Later generations were also affected, as dioxins were transmitted through the food chain and the environment.

From a military perspective, the operations succeeded in temporarily reducing vegetation cover and making Viet Cong operations more difficult. However, the human and environmental costs were vastly disproportionate to the military benefits gained.

The tests primarily affected civilians, including women, children, and the elderly, who had no direct link to the conflict. The use of chemical weapons in civilian-inhabited areas raises serious ethical questions about the conduct of war and respect for human rights.

Details about the use of chemical weapons in Vietnam became more widely known in the decades following the war. Public awareness of the ethical aspects and consequences of these actions led to increased scrutiny of military and research policies.

The chemical weapons tests in Vietnam contributed to the evolution of international regulations on the use of chemical weapons. Treaties such as the Chemical Weapons Convention were developed in part as a response to these and similar atrocities.

21. Contraceptive Experiments in Puerto Rico

During the 1950s, contraceptive experiments were conducted in Puerto Rico. These studies, which involved the use of the first oral contraceptive pill, were conducted with the goal of evaluating its efficacy and safety. However, the tests raised serious ethical questions related to the side effects experienced by the participants.

In the 1950s, researchers were looking for effective contraceptive methods to control population growth and improve women's reproductive health. The invention of the oral contraceptive pill was seen as a revolutionary advance, but it needed to be tested in clinical trials to evaluate its efficacy and safety.

Puerto Rico was chosen as the test site due to several reasons: the high birth rate, the population density, and the fact that the island was under U.S. control, which made it easier to conduct the studies. In addition, the predominantly poor and working-class population was seen as an ideal sample for the experiments.

Study participants were mostly poor women from Puerto Rico, many of whom were not fully informed about the experimental nature of the birth control pills they were given. Women were enrolled in the studies through local family planning clinics.

Experimental Procedures:

<u>Pill Administration:</u> Women received daily doses of the birth control pill, which contained high concentrations of hormones.

<u>Monitoring for Side Effects:</u> Researchers monitored participants for side effects, including nausea, vomiting, headaches, and other symptoms.

<u>Evaluating Efficacy:</u> The effectiveness of the pill in preventing pregnancy was evaluated throughout the study.

Results were carefully documented, and the data collected was used to adjust the pill's formulation to reduce its side effects.

The studies showed that the birth control pill was highly effective in preventing pregnancy. However, the initial high hormonal dose caused numerous adverse side effects in participants, including:

• Nausea and vomiting
• Headaches
• Dizziness
• Menstrual problems

Some side effects were serious but were often downplayed or ignored in initial reports.

Despite the controversies, the data collected from these studies was instrumental in the development and improvement of the birth control pill, which later became a widely used and revolutionary birth control method.

One of the main criticisms of these studies was that many women were not fully informed about the experimental nature of the pills, the associated risks, and possible side effects.

The use of poor and working-class women in Puerto Rico, who had less access to medical information and resources, raises serious ethical concerns about exploitation and fairness in medical research.

The details of the contraceptive experiments in Puerto Rico became more widely known in subsequent decades, generating outrage and criticism toward the research practices used.

Despite the controversies, the studies provided crucial data that helped improve the birth control pill, which has had a lasting impact on women's reproductive health around the world.

22. Nutritional Experimentation on Indigenous Children

During the 1940s and 1950s, the Canadian government conducted nutritional experiments on indigenous children without their or their parents' consent. These studies were conducted in residential schools and indigenous communities with the aim of evaluating the impact of various nutritional deficiencies and supplements. The research, which involved deliberate nutrient deprivation and supplementation, had devastating effects on children's health and raised serious ethical questions.

For much of the 20th century, the Canadian government implemented policies that sought to assimilate indigenous populations, often through coercive methods. Residential schools, which sought to eliminate indigenous cultures and assimilate children into Euro-Canadian society, played a central role in these policies.

Canada's indigenous communities faced severe nutritional problems due to poverty, discrimination, and government policies that restricted their access to traditional foods. These problems were particularly evident in residential schools, where food quality was poor and malnutrition was widespread.

Nutritional experiments were conducted in several residential schools and indigenous communities. Participants were selected without their consent and without adequately informing their parents about the nature of the studies.

Experimental Procedures:

<u>Nutrient Deprivation:</u> In some studies, children were denied access to certain essential nutrients to observe the effects of nutritional deficiency.

<u>Nutritional Supplements:</u> In other studies, nutritional supplements were given to children to assess their impact on health and growth.

Researchers monitored the children's health and development, recording data on their growth, health status, and other biological indicators.

The results of the studies were meticulously documented, and the data collected was used to write scientific reports and articles.

The experiments had devastating effects on the children's health. Deprivation of essential nutrients caused serious health problems, including:

• Growth and developmental delays
• Diseases related to nutritional deficiency
• Cognitive and learning problems
• Evaluation of Nutritional Supplements

Studies involving the administration of nutritional supplements demonstrated that supplements could improve the health of children, but these results were often achieved at the expense of the health of other children who were deprived of nutrients.

Despite the controversies, the studies provided important data on the impact of nutrition on child health and development, although these data were obtained in deeply immoral and unethical ways.

A major criticism of these studies was that children and their parents were not informed about the experimental nature of the studies, the risks involved, or the objectives of the studies.

The use of Indigenous children, who were already in a vulnerable position due to government policies and discrimination, raises serious ethical concerns about exploitation and fairness in medical research.

Details of nutritional experiments on Indigenous children became more widely known in later decades, sparking outrage and criticism of the research practices used.

Nutritional experiments on Indigenous children in Canada during the 1940s and 1950s represent a controversial and complex chapter in the history of medical research. While they contributed to the scientific understanding of nutrition, they also raised serious ethical questions about the consent and treatment of participants.

23. Biological Weapons Experiments in San Francisco

In 1950, the US Navy conducted a series of experiments known as "Operation Sea-Spray" in San Francisco, California, in which they released bacteria to study the vulnerability of American cities to biological attacks.

During the Cold War, the United States stepped up its research into biological weapons as part of its defense strategy. Fear of a biological attack by the Soviet Union prompted the military to study the vulnerability of American cities to such attacks.

San Francisco was chosen for its climate, population density, and geographic location, making it an ideal location to test the dispersion of biological agents.

The US Navy used Serratia marcescens, a bacterium that was believed to be harmless at the time, and Bacillus globigii, which was commonly used in biological tests because of its similarity to more dangerous agents.

Experimental Procedures:

Bacteria Release: Bacteria were released from ships located near the coast of San Francisco using aerosols.

Dispersal Monitoring: Researchers monitored the dispersal of bacteria throughout the city using several sampling stations.

Data Collection: Data was collected on the presence of bacteria in different areas of the city to assess dispersal efficiency and population exposure.

Results were carefully documented, and the data collected was used to write scientific reports and studies on vulnerability to biological attacks.

The experiments demonstrated that bacteria could be efficiently dispersed over large areas, exposing a large portion of the population to biological agents without people realizing it.

After the release of the bacteria, several cases of respiratory infections and illnesses were recorded. One man, Edward Nevin, died from an infection caused by Serratia marcescens, prompting an investigation into the cause of his illness and the relationship to the experiments.

The studies provided valuable information about the dispersion of biological agents and the vulnerability of cities, although they were carried out at the expense of the health and well-being of citizens.

It should be noted that the citizens of San Francisco were not informed about the nature of the studies or the risks associated with the release of bacteria.

The use of a civilian population for biological warfare experiments raises serious ethical concerns about exploitation and fairness in research.

The details of the experiments were kept secret for many years. In the 1970s, information about

"Operation Sea-Spray" was declassified, leading to outrage and criticism of the research practices used.

24. Radioactive Contamination Studies in Uranium Miners

During the 1950s and 1960s, studies were conducted to assess the effects of radiation exposure on uranium miners in the United States, particularly in the southwestern regions. These studies, conducted without proper consent and with limited knowledge of the risks involved, revealed elevated rates of lung cancer and other serious illnesses among miners.

Between 1950 and 1960, demand for uranium skyrocketed due to the development of nuclear weapons and nuclear power. This led to a significant expansion of uranium mining, especially in the southwestern United States.

Working conditions in uranium mines were extremely harsh and dangerous. Miners, many of whom were Native Americans or immigrant workers, were exposed to high levels of radiation without adequate protection.

The studies were conducted on uranium miners working in various mines across the United States. Many of these workers were not adequately informed about the risks they faced or the nature of the studies.

Experimental Procedures:

<u>Radiation Monitoring:</u> Radiation levels in the mines and the miners' exposure were monitored using dosimeters and other measurement techniques.

<u>Medical Examinations:</u> Periodic medical examinations were conducted to assess the miners' health, focusing especially on lung function and cancer incidence.

<u>Data Collection</u>: Data on radiation exposure and miners' health were collected and analyzed to identify correlations and trends.

The results of the studies were documented in scientific reports and articles, although the risks to the miners were often underestimated or ignored.

The studies revealed significantly elevated rates of lung cancer and other respiratory diseases among uranium miners. Long-term exposure to radon and radioactive dust in the mines was identified as the main cause of these health problems.

The research showed that radioactive contamination in uranium mines was much greater than had been anticipated and that safety measures were inadequate to protect workers.

Although the studies provided crucial information about the effects of radiation on human health, they were conducted at the expense of the health and well-being of the miners.

Over time, details of the studies and the risks associated with uranium mining became more widely known, leading to outrage and demands for justice for the affected miners.

The studies contributed to the evolution of regulations on workplace safety and worker protection, leading to a greater emphasis on mine safety and compensation for affected workers.

25. Experimentation with Lobotomy Surgery

Lobotomy, a form of surgery that involves the destruction or alteration of parts of the brain, was a common practice in the treatment of mental illness during the 1940s and 1950s.

Lobotomy was introduced as a revolutionary treatment for various mental illnesses, including schizophrenia and severe depression. However, its indiscriminate application and devastating results for many patients have made this practice a symbol of the dangers of unregulated medicine and human experimentation.

Lobotomy was developed by Portuguese neurologist António Egas Moniz in the 1930s. Moniz believed that certain behaviors and mental disorders could be treated by destroying nerve connections in the frontal lobe of the brain.

American neurosurgeon Walter Freeman, along with his colleague James W. Watts, popularized lobotomy in the United States. Freeman developed a less invasive method known as transorbital lobotomy, which could be performed quickly without the need for a fully equipped operating room.

Experimental Procedures:

Prefrontal Lobotomy: This technique involves drilling into the skull and severing the connections between the frontal lobes and the rest of the brain.

Transorbital Lobotomy: Developed by Freeman, this technique involved inserting an ice-pick-like instrument through the eye socket to access and alter the frontal lobe.

Patients selected for lobotomy included those with schizophrenia, severe depression, chronic anxiety, and other mental illnesses who were unresponsive to other treatments. Often, patients did not have the capacity to give informed consent due to the severity of their mental illness.

The results of lobotomies were varied. While some patients showed improvements in certain symptoms, many others suffered devastating side effects, such as personality changes, cognitive impairment, and in some cases, death.

Clinical Outcomes:

<u>Successes:</u> Some patients experienced a reduction in anxiety and agitation symptoms, allowing them to better integrate socially.

<u>Failure and Harms:</u> Many patients suffered serious side effects, including apathy, lack of initiative, loss of cognitive function, and childlike behavior.

Lobotomy was initially seen as an advance in psychiatry, but over time it became an example of inhumane treatment and misunderstanding of mental illness. The practice of lobotomy declined dramatically with the introduction of antipsychotic medications in the 1950s.

A major criticism was the lack of adequate informed consent. Many patients and their families did not fully understand the risks and consequences of lobotomy.

Lobotomy was used indiscriminately on a wide variety of patients, including children and people with minor disabilities, without adequate assessment of the benefits and risks.

The practice disproportionately affected vulnerable populations, including the poor and those in mental institutions, who were less able to refuse treatment.

As the devastating effects of lobotomy became known, the practice came under increasing criticism from both the public and the medical community.

The controversies surrounding lobotomy led to increased regulation of psychiatric treatments and increased protection of patients' rights. This included the introduction of informed consent procedures and the ethical review of medical practices.

Although lobotomy is today considered an inhumane procedure, it provided valuable insights into brain function and the relationship between certain areas of the brain and behavior.

_______O_______

Other books by the author Phillips Tahuer that you will find on this platform:

- The greatest conspiracy theories
- Great robberies in history
- Famous murderers - the evil side of the mind-
- Lives in captivity - Stories of real kidnappings-
- Agents, informants, and traitors - the world of espionage-
- Pirates of the 21st century
- Tragic loves
- 30 curiosities of World War II
- Dark experiments on humans
- Real-life heroes
- Powerful men in history modern
- Valentine's Day Stories
- Lessons in Practical Psychology